T0157001

"SPIRIT"

SPIRIT'S VIRTUAL WORLD

PEGGY D'AMATO

Order this book online at www.trafford.com
or email orders@trafford.com

Most Trafford titles are also available at major online book retailers.

Print information available on the last page.

ISBN: 978-1-4907-9055-8 (sc)
ISBN: 978-1-4907-9056-5 (e)

Trafford rev. 08/24/2018

 www.trafford.com

North America & international
toll-free: 1 888 232 4444 (USA & Canada)
fax: 812 355 4082

DEDICATED TO

Animal & Pet Lovers
Around the World

and

A Special Dedication To

Nickolas
A Very Special Young Man
&
Dexter
Nick's Dog

Introduction

$\mathcal{S}$PIRIT, is a moving, exciting, mystical story about a very intelligent dog! A dog named Spirit. A dog that lived a full life doing compassionate services for the elderly, sick and dying in hospice care. A touching story about the unconditional love of a pet! A dog with an extensive vocabulary, that understood English, Spanish, Greek and a bit of Italian as well.

The Greeks knew of the many different kinds of love, which they had a name for them all. Love of God, of family, of art, music, nature. But the name for the unconditional love a pet gives a human, is called Caritas love. Caritas is an exceedingly great forgiving love, inconceivable, being of an eternal nature, having no boundaries, is an eternal round.

As humans we often love with conditions, our dogs love us without limits. Their love is not dependent on conditions or learning. Their love is devoted and loyal to their masters until their final day, or ours, in this physical world. I believe, this unconditional love and loyalty our pets possess, go beyond the virtual veil of this physical world, across the veil, where the virtual spiritual form, of all existence, of divergent rays of light continue to exist, for all eternity. Like an image is seen in a plane mirror, being in essence or effect, but not in fact, but nevertheless, it is that it is! Mystical, magical, mystifying!

LOVE, unconditionally, is what our animals, pets, be it a dog, cat, bird, even an elephant, give to us. A love, which will continue on the other side. Like the circle or ring, so is eternity, an eternal round! If you cut the ring and break this circle, you still will have no beginning or end, for who is to say which is which! To have faith, to believe, gives us the comfort to know, they love and wait for us eternally, on the other side of Heavens Portal.

SPIRIT

CHAPTER I

Puppies in The Window

It all started one day when I went shopping for a new pair of tennis shoes. I was walking in Fashion Center Shopping Mall, in Scottsdale, Arizona, on the second floor where the shoe store was. When I got off the elevator, I immediately noticed a smell, that of a pet store! I was quit curious as to why I would smell a pet shop in the mall, as I had never noticed any pet stores in the past in any malls. But after all, this was 2004 and times had changed since I had bought my pets in the previous years.

In the years past, I had owned several cats in my youth, as well as many parakeets, as many children do, as well as lots of dogs. Usually two dogs at a time, lest one would get lonely, or in the event one would pass away, I would still have another one to give me that "unconditional love" that pets afford we humans. Dogs, cats, birds, many pets become devoted to their owners, with loyalty unsurpassed. Thus, the reason so many of us love our pets as much, if not at times more than people! They are really family! Anyone who has lost a pet knows the heartache is really equal to that loss of a family member. Love has no borders or boundaries, with devoted pets, they do not see race, color or creed. Isn't that a wonderful thought! If only we humans could be more like them when it comes to unconditional love, the world would be a better place for sure.

After getting off the elevator, I turned to my right to locate the shoe store and immediately heard the sound of puppies barking. Oh what a pleasant sound, tiny little barks drawing me towards that pet shop, just next door, right before the shoe store. Adorable little puppies in front window dressing, running back and forth in the window, which was a window about 15 feet long. Three dainty, cute little puppies playing with each other, running back and forth, one chewing on a teddy bear toy in the window. I decided to just go in and ask if I could hold one, I had no intentions of buying a puppy that day, absolutely none. I had just lost one of my two dogs recently, leaving me with just my little black dog, with a white breast, named "Baby". Baby looked just like a little "penguin", with his little short legs and white breast, was about the size of a penguin too. Baby was 16 years old and was 90 percent blind, weighted in at 7 pounds. He had learned to follow his younger sister's shadow image. Being 90 percent blind, his sister had become his eyes, so he always followed her closely. His legs being shorter than hers, he had to run to keep in step with her. Taffy, was a beautiful silver and white poodle, weighed in at 12 lbs. She became ill when she was only 7 years old. When I took her to her vet, he told me, she had tumors, that they would get a lot worse and suggested I put her down when her breathing became bad. I remember asking him, how will I know when that is, he replied, you will know. When Taffy was 8 years young, I made that awful decision to take her to her vet. I returned home alone to her little blind brother. I cried for weeks over the loss of Taffy. My heart hurt deeply that Baby had no shadow to follow any longer, how would he manage now? Manage he did, as he followed me step by step, everywhere I walked. He didn't even need a leash, as he never allowed me out of his dim lit vision. I had taken his sisters place it seemed. But he seemed sad and slept more often than before we lost Taffy.

I decided the shoes could wait a few extra minutes, I would see what this new pet shop in closed in mall had to offer, maybe find some special treats for Baby, and of course hold a new puppy, that is always such fun. I walked into the

pet store, walked to the center counter, but all
the clerks were so busy I couldn't ask to hold a
new puppy, so I decided to walk around the store
and look in the glass cages at the other puppies,
checking out the toys and treats. I watched a
family in a small room with one of the puppies
playing, they were deciding if they wanted
that puppy, it looked like a baby bear, cute as a
button. Then I walked to the very back of the
store, it appeared that one cage with a glass front
was full of black and white paper, all shredded
into strips, which was obviously news paper
shredding.

A clerk finally came over to me at this time,
asking if she could help me. I asked her where
was this puppy, as the cage looked empty. She
said, oh that puppy is hiding, she is somewhere
under the shredded news papers. I asked if I
could hold that one, why I don't know! She said
of course, wait here and I will go to the back and
get her out for you. The clerk told me I would
need to go into the little room to hold her, so I
said ok and followed the clerk. She asked me to
sit down first. I did. But I still did not see the
puppy, as she had it covered the tiny puppy with
her apron, which she had lifted up and over the
puppy. She also sat down, with puppy still held
tightly within her apron, wiggling to and fro,
twisting and turning in her apron!

I began to wonder what kind of puppy is so wiggle that it would require covering up in an apron to even show me the puppy, and would I ever get to see this particular puppy. I was already having second thoughts! Maybe I picked the wrong puppy to hold! But my curiosity about this unrevealed little secret creature aroused my desire to know, what it looked like, what kind of puppy could not be, just held and shown to me! It was quietly removed from the black and white news papers, quickly gathered up in a sales clerks apron, walked into a little viewing room, and I still hadn't had a single glance at this busy wiggling little creature!

Well, now finally, I am going to see this puppy, I thought! But, nope, not yet, as the clerk had to first introduce herself to me and tell me a little bit about the puppy, as she continued to keep the puppy tightly held within her apron. My mouth fell open, I began to laugh, as I explained to the clerk how funny I found it to be that this puppy was being held so tightly. She smiled and told me her name was Tammy, and the puppy was a fifth generation full pedigree poodle, with show dog qualities, from a history of race dogs! I said, really, that's nice! Sounds really special. She continued, it's mom was named "Tiny Comet", her mom was named "Star". I replied, that's nice, Comet, really! Tammy continued telling me how fast all the family history was, even pro track racers. I said, really, fast, really!! By now my mouth was half way to the floor, wondering when she was going to put the dog down and let me at least see it! I really had no intentions of buying a puppy this day and began to feel bad for the nice clerk going to all this trouble to explain all the history of this little pedigree race dog. So I apologized and explained to her that I was just curious as to what the puppy looked like since I couldn't see it under all the news papers. Tammy then warned me, that she would have to bend over and put the puppy down on the floor for me to see her, as she was a wiggle worm. Tammy said she did not want to drop the puppy when she opened her apron. My mouth was still wide open waiting to see what kind of dog could possibly be such an issue! Then suddenly as the apron unfolds, in a blink of an eye, a puppy jumps out and over my leg, running in circles so fast that I couldn't see her face at all! I was in total shock! What in hell is that, I thought to myself, I can't see it's face, it's eyes are covered with a mask of black. I could see it's eyes sparkle, but it moved so fast I couldn't figure out what she really looked like. She looked like a raccoon running around the room. But was a white poodle, with a black mask, with a black tail, looked like a black and white snowball out of hell. I tried to grab her over and over, unsuccessfully! She would slip right out of my hands, I was amazed at how flexible and fast this tiny puppy was. I thought to myself, her mom was Tiny Comet! Go figure! Tammy said, let her run a while and she will maybe let you pick her up. Maybe! You have got to be kidding I boldly stated to Tammy. Tammy must have shown her a lot, as she patiently waited for the puppy to just stop. We just sat there for a few minutes watching her run the tiny room, darting from corner to corner, in and out from under our chairs. She was like lightning, faster than even my eyes could keep up with her. She would be in one corner and then another corner before I could even see from one point to another! Shocked and amazed at her I waited for her to stop, as Tammy reassured me she would. Suddenly, she stopped dead still, breathing fast with her tiny tongue hanging out. I started to reach down and there she went again. Tammy kept reassuring me she would stop, but to just let her know I did not intend to pick her up! What I thought! But isn't that why I was in this little room, to hold the puppy, right?! Again I thought, you have got to be kidding, I don't want this dog for sure, she will drive me nuts running, I am so glad I am not really looking to buy a puppy today, I thought! Then she stopped again, sat down and looked at me, straight in the eyes! She really looked like a raccoon, with that black mask across her eyes and around her ears. Tammy said she is a phantom parti poodle. I replied, oh, like

"Phantom of the Opera", a little spooky huh! That she is for sure, like a ghost or spirit, she is so fast.

This strange little fast comet finally decided to stop running, but each time I put my hand down to her little nose, she would smell and look at me, as soon as she thought I was going to pick her up, she darted away, backed up, jumped straight up in the air, like a jumping bean! Just as I was ready to give up and say goodbye, she wagged her silly little black tail, lay down, rolled over kicking. Tammy tickled her tummy. Oh, that's how it works, ok, I tickled her tummy for a few minutes, she wanted more tickles, as she wiggled around in circles on the floor. Then in a dash she turns over and put her tiny front paws on my ankle, wagging her tail. I slowly bent over to gently pick her up, which she allowed me to do, but before I could get her higher than my knees, she flew like a bird from my hands. Tammy was worried I could see, that she might hurt herself jumping from me. I continued to pet her on the floor for a bit and decided it was time to leave, when she decided to try one more time to be my friend, jumping up and down like a "yoyo" on my feet, she gently put her soft little paws on my ankle again. Once again I gently picked her up, very very slowly, put her on my knees, petting her. I put her down, and repeated the game over again, she would not let me hold her in my arms, rather only on my knees, so I bent over to her face and she gave me little kisses. I thought what a strange attraction I have for this little mini raccoon! I was curious how much this little doggie in the window, but not the show window, cost, so I asked Tammy her price. Tammy said she is a pedigree and a rare breed, so is a bit of a high priced puppy, since you can breed her, you know! As she declared, $1,700.00! My eyes wide open, I said, don't think I ever held a dog this expensive, and well, still haven't it seems! She laughed, as I continued explaining that I wasn't into breeding dogs, nor was I interested in her being a pedigree, I'm just looking for a puppy to keep my other dog happy.

I was out of time and had to run, so I thanked Tammy and stated, I will call you when she goes on sale, she is a bit out of my price range. Tammy said, she has been here too long already, chances are she will be half price soon. I said, how soon? Tammy replied, probably in a month or even less.

For some reason I couldn't get that puppy out of my head and I saw my old dog sad and not long for the world. I decided to call Tammy a about three weeks later. Tammy said the puppy is now half price, but she was transferred to one of our less expensive pet stores in another city! I said, where, she replied Chandler, Arizona. Tammy gave me the phone number of the Chandler Pet Store, I called immediately and told them I was on my way to pick up the puppy Tammy gave me the registration number for. They said not a problem, she is here.

When I saw her again for that second time, in that small glass cage, in another store, I felt sad for her, because I had caused her to spend almost an extra month sitting in a cage all alone, on sale, and no body wanted her, even on sale. It broke my heart, as I had hoped someone would have paid the full price to have this puppy.

It was so sad to know what she had already been through, and of course I wondered why she feared being held, maybe she had been dropped, maybe more than once, maybe she was even hurting, injured. I would never really know since she couldn't talk to me, to tell me those secrets only she knew. But I knew, once I took her home with me she would be ok, and nobody would ever drop her again.

I did not even bother to ask to hold this dear puppy, it felt really strange getting my check book out to buy a new puppy that never even let me hold her! But somehow I knew this animal was special for me, I knew she somehow was sent, in a spiritual matter, just for me, because I would need her in the years to come in my life. In the years to come this puppy would prove to have been heaven sent!

A puppy, that looked like a little mini raccoon, half price, full pedigree, bargain puppy, that was hidden in shredded news papers. A puppy that didn't want to be held, I thought, as I wrote the check!

Of course that was just the beginning of costs, we had to have a baby crib to keep her from running all over the house until potty trained. I had done this many times before, had it all figured out, the doggie door always worked for all the other dogs, she will be a quick learner, I figured! She was very quick, but had been such a fast learner, learning to potty on her wee wee pads, in the corner of her baby crib, that she did not feel using a doggie door was needed to wee wee, just poo poo! Weird, this animal required two separate places it seemed to potty. So, first things first, she was given her very own bath room, in the master bed room. Extra large pee pee pads were placed in the huge shower, where I could use the shower head to clean and wash the area down each week. This remained her bathroom for her life, she never made one mistake ever in the home!

Now since I really believed she was heaven sent, I felt the best name for her would be SPIRIT. I once heard of a race horse being named Spirit, but never a dog, plus she was so mystical with that mask across her face, yes, Spirit is a good name for this special puppy I thought, sent to me from heaven above.

I wrote the check for all her new things, and the clerk had placed her new "body" leash firmly around this wild little thing. I tried not to think of the trip home in the car with her, but to my amazement she was calm, sat in her new crib in the front seat, with her body leash tied to the side of the crib. As the years went by I learned that Spirit would be the best traveling dog I ever had. She was never afraid of anything with wheels, even a wheel chair she looked at as having a ride!

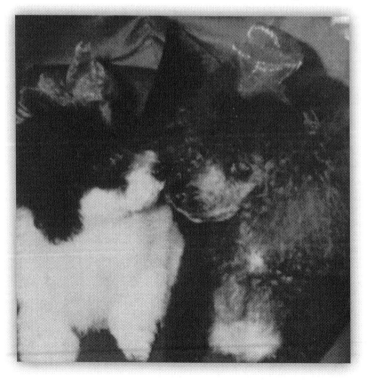

Spirit and Baby

I was hoping and praying that she and my old dog, Baby, would get along well, as I drove towards home with my new puppy. When we arrived, Spirit immediately smelled her new friend, not understanding exactly why this new brother just sat still as she tried to play with him. At first Baby was nervous, because he was not accustomed to such an active runner in the house as Spirit was. He was accustomed to his sister, Taffy, the calm sister. But come evening Baby knew the new puppy had to sleep in her own crib, he was safe as he slept on the bench at the foot of mommy's bed. This seemed to be working just fine, until the smart little puppy figured things out one evening! Spirit decided this just wasn't fair, she wanted out of the crib and decided to get out! To my amazement Spirit, using her talent of high jumping, jumping out of that crib, onto the bench at the foot of mommy's bed, and lay down next to Baby. Baby had to be lifted each night to her bed on the bench, and carried outside now, as her vision was so bad. This was a very difficult time for all of us.

My dad had passed away the year before, as well as my late husband, so my dear sweet mom moved in with me. She had also lost her companion, a Pekinese dog named Panda Bear a few years prior, so she was thrilled to have both dogs. Although, Spirit was a bit much at times, as she learned the floor plan of the house, she would run like the speed of light, throughout the house, in a pattern. The pattern was always the same, thank heaven, as she had learned, she could run faster if she had a certain pattern. Like a dart, she would fly throughout the house! Mom and I knew to just stand still, not to move as she flew through her pattern, which lasted generally two to three minutes. We feared she would run into the wall or break a leg, but it never happened.

Baby was inactive now, so he didn't care! He was blind, he couldn't see her swiftly streaking about him, so made him no difference. A couple of times I thought about the possibility of Spirit causing my mom to maybe trip over her, or even fall, if Spirit ran into her cane by accident. I decided it was time to mom about it, telling her I was worried about her, when I wasn't home. After all mom was now 83 years old. Mom said not to worry, my brain still works just fine, and I don't plan on getting in the way of Spirit, she exclaimed firmly! Nevertheless, I am concerned I said. Mother sat down on her bed side, in her bedroom, with a serious look, on her still pretty face, with her ageing body that ached from persistent pain. She patted her bed, gently looked at me and said, now sit down, I have something serious to say, and I don't want to have to say this twice. Well I knew whatever she had to say, she had obviously given it serious thought, or she wouldn't have said sit down, so I sat down. Mom patted my knee, as she looked down to her bad knee, rubbing it. She said, my child, you are the only child I ever had, you are a widow, without any children, you may decide that you never want to remarry, you will need Spirit, do you understand? I said I do understand, I thanked her for her love and deep concern. She continued by telling me how I was like my grandmother, strong willed, independent and self reliant, and talked a bit about what an amazing history of women I come from. I learned a lot by listening to her stories about grandma, owning the largest chicken ranch in the city, farming and raising animals. About out houses, wells for water, no electricity, living through the great depression, trying to feed six hungry children, while living in the barn, because the family estate burned to the ground. I told her I did remember the big barn well, because grandpa was a carpenter and let me play in the big old barn while he worked. She went on to explain why I needed to keep Spirit, because, when the time comes, that she and Baby leave me in this world, I won't be home alone, I will have Spirit, with her unconditional love and companionship, she promised and assured me, repeating you will need Spirit.

How true those words were, spoken to me from a wise old woman, my very special loving mother!

Less than a year later Baby passed away. I hardly could get over his loss, when, within a year of his passing, my mom spent the rest of her life either going into surgery, in the hospital, back home, back into the hospitals, and into a rest home, passing away in the care of Hospice. Spirit was always by my side, what a comfort she was, just as mom had promised she would be. Life without mom would be different now. Mom was right, it would be me and Spirit alone, for 5 years to be exact.

And, during those years we lived in the house alone, we developed ways to stay busy, have fun, work together and travel on wheels, lots of wheeling!

It took me a while before I realized that after 26 years of married life, I stopped hearing from my married friends, they stopped inviting me to come to their homes for dinner! For a few years, I thought it was just because they were so busy, or because I was so busy with my mom, but they never called to invite me out when I wasn't busy! Finally, one of the members of "the church", I "was" a member of, explained to me "how the cow ate the cabbage", so as to speak! One evening when I attempted to sit down next to her at a dinner table, in church, for the annual Thanksgiving Dinner. It was a table for 10 in the round, there were over 25 tables of 10, I knew the singles sat together and married couples sat with married couples, but I never made friends with the singles, as I never planned to stay single long! So, I attempted to sit next to Vonda, at one of the beautifully set table for 10, she quickly stated, "you can't sit next to me", that is reserved for Tom! Tom was her husband, which was the brother to my friend, as well as my doctor. Matter of fact, doc was married to my best friend! We were all close, I thought! Vonda continued, you will need to find the tables where the single people sit together, you are single now, you can't sit between my husband and I, now can you?? I said, of course not! I will sit across the table, how is that? I was in shock, as this was, I thought one of my best friends. As fate would have it, Tom left Vonda, moved to Prescott and remarried, his brother divorced his wife also! And, I did move, and never tried to befriend married couples again, nor did I ever go to another church dinner. I became very single, and did not like that, but, Spirit and I made some great friends along the way of being single, a few are still friends today. Angie and Faith, which are still single. I learned a lot from these independent survivors swimming with sharks. Angie was an RN working with military veterans with many health issues, including PTSD, she didn't have a pet at all, so took to Spirit and Spirit loved her. Faith was also an amazing woman, and a shared love for dogs, she still has two at this time, they played together with my Spirit, when our puppies were all younger. Other than Faith and Angie, single friends are few, as most single women do finally get married or remarried, or re-remarried! Beginning a new circle of life for them once again, as they move on in life with their new partners, as it should be.

As the years passed I looked for a husband, and finally found one, just for me, not of my faith, but that did not concern me anymore, as long as he and I agreed that we shared a belief in the same God, had some of the same interests, as well as agreeing to love my little girl, Spirit, as I did.

Spirit was definitely a big priority, since she was devoted to me when I was alone. Any partner I should choose would have to accept her! I knew Spirit would be devoted to any man I was devoted to. I realized the fact that dogs, cats, any pets can be a "deal breaker"! As I had broken off a relationship with a really nice guy, due to his dog! Sam had a beautiful 230 lb., English Mastiff dog, two cats, 5 horses, and a yard full of rattlesnakes at his desert home in Cave Creek, Arizona! Not even a million $ dollars could fix that! Spirit was a small poodle, loved running, but not with 25 lb. diamondback rattlers in the drive way! Walking her at night meant wearing boots, caring a light and a gun!

Data is that Arizona sees as many as 350 rattlesnake bite cases (kill many) each year. Between 7,000 and 8,000 people are bitten by venomous snakes in the U.S. every year! According to WHO (World Health Organization), in 2008 (10 years ago), the systematic review of worldwide snakebite literature, it was estimated that each year over 400,000 human snakebites occur, with at least 20,000 deaths.

Sad story was told July 2, 2018 (UPI) news, about an Arizona woman branded her golden retriever her "hero", after the puppy jumped between her and a rattlesnake strike, the snake bit the beautiful golden retriever puppy in the face. Headlines "Arizona puppy takes rattlesnake bite to save owner! News reports a lot about human bites from deadly snakes, but not a lot of record keeping when it comes to the number of pet deaths due to a snake bites.

After breaking off the engagement with Sam, the deal breaker, due to our dogs, animals, and snake issues, I was sad to learn from a mutual friend, his beautiful English Mastiff dog, named "Hummer" was bitten by a snake, while with a neighbor, when Sam was out of town. Hummer was found outside in a hole he obviously dug for himself.

It is said, some dogs know when they are going to die, and they seek a place for this purpose! When you think about this, ask yourself how many animals and birds that die naturally, do you ever really see drop dead? A bird dies, where? I never buried a wild bird, just my parakeets! The wild seem to just disappear, like magic! Amazing!

We once had a wild owl, for 20 plus years, here at our home. We saw it often in our 60 ft. pine tree, in our front yard. Mom was alive then.

Mom and I would take Spirit outside at sunset, sit under the giant pine, in our lawn chairs, on the lush green grass, waiting to see the owl at sunset. Mom said it was called an Arizona "Burrowing Owl", which live underground, but they would hunt at sunset. The owl used the pine tree to spot prey. We would see her everyday about the same time, at sunset. She was spotted with light gray coloring, bit of stripes, large yellow eyes, with large black centers and white eyebrows. We named her Athena, after the Greek goddess of the night, the goddess of wisdom. She was interesting and very social, wise old owl. She hooted at us from the pine tree, turning her pretty little head sideways, looking us with one of her big yellow eyes, with white eyebrows. Mom hooted back her, having a regular conversation, Spirit stayed very quiet, looking up at Athena, then at mom "hooting". I often wondered what Spirit was thinking when mom "hooted"!

We fell in love with Athena, as we saw her so often, she really knew us. One day when she was in the pine tree, after mom passed away, Spirit and I continued the ritual at sunset. As we walked around in the grassy area, a very large area where the pine tree stood, Athena was grooming her feathers, when we noticed one feather, about 10 inches long, all fluffy, floating down in front of us. It was from her wing as she groomed her feathers. Spirit ran over to retrieve it for me.

I am an artist, and love to paint the stars and galaxies. I needed something better than a paint brush to paint stars! I suddenly realized, Athena was giving me a message! She must have known I needed that feather! I love to watch the stars, she knew this, after all she watched us watching those stars regularly! I later used Athena's feather to paint thousands of stars, in many of my paintings. The feather was so unique, as it had a tiny hole in the center of the feather which turned out to work wonders to dot stars into the night sky paintings.

Spirit and I enjoyed our night skies, always looking for the brightest star, "Sirius", which the brightest star in the Earth's night sky, also known as the "Dog Star", it means "glowing" in Greek. Sirius is known as the Dog Star, because it's the chief star in the constellation Canis Major, the Big Dog!

One sunset evening, we no longer saw Athena, or heard her hoots! Sitting under the old pine tree, just wasn't the same any more, without mom or Athena!

Spirit and I had gone through a lot of losses together. But we continued life, kept finding adventure in her world together. What a total blessing this creature of heaven was for me, with her companionship and unconditional love!

The Old Greyhound
Chance

CHAPTER II

Spirit Meets Chance

NOW, Spirit and I had to make a new life for ourselves, now that we lost everyone in our family, in our small corner of the world! It was time for travel and lots of adventure. It was, as mom said, Spirit and I would have each other. What a blessing Spirit was to me at this time in my life!

I was not retired and my work travel, we drove a lot out of the city. Spirit loved to travel and was a great travel companion. She was trained at the Dog and Puppy Training School for behavior, temperament, and obedience commands. A quick learner, smart and very obedient. Therefore, she was welcomed wherever I traveled. Often it was in a large manufacturing plant for cement or cattle and feed lots. I sold petroleum products for high temperature areas in these plants, these customers did not care at all if my dog followed me around the area of the feed lots or plants. At times she patiently waited in the car for me, sometimes the secretary in the general office would baby sit. They loved to baby sit Spirit, but knew never to pick her up, as she only allowed me to do this. She was trained not to take treats from strangers as well, so she refused all treats, to others amazement!

Spirit loved those trips, especially when I had to visit customers in northern Arizona, we would stay in a cabin on the creek in Sedona, Arizona. For such a lively dog, she had amazing fortitude and patience! She could sit on the front porch at the cabin and watch the rabbits and birds for hours on end. Funny, she never barked at them, she just watched them, with her nose in the air, smelling the trees and rushing water, as it rolled over the huge rocks below our cabin. Spirit was more observant than any pet I had owned in the past, as she was not a dog that barked unless she had a reason or wanted to let me know something. Her watching birds, rather than barking at them, studying the rabbits, not chasing the rabbits was different, on a different level than other dogs. Although, if she considered the animal a threat to us, she would give a warning growl, bark if they moved to close without permission!

Spirit never barked at the cows on the grain lots, rather she found them quite amusing, as there were thousands of head of cattle in the feed lots behind the fenced in areas, I would actually walk her to the fence to watch them, as most people know cows, herds, are as curious about us, as we are about them! The herds would moo, causing the entire herd to moo, as they walked closer towards us, to see us! Spirit never barked at them, but her nose would go up in the air, sniffing as her ears moved up and down in her virtual world. She could see, hear and smell the cows, even a taste was in the air due to the grain elevators! What fun to enjoy this journey together, it was a real adventure with her at times!

The plant manager of the feed lot was Bill. He had adopted a beautiful retired Greyhound dog, named Chance. Chance was an Italian Greyhound, weighing in at 13 pounds and standing about 15 inches tall at the top of his shoulder. The Italian greyhound is considered the "toy" of greyhounds. They have a deep chest, long slender legs, a long neck that tapers down to a small head. The head is long and pointed, like a full sized greyhound. Overall, they look like "miniature" greyhounds. But they are true genetic greyhounds, with bloodline extending back over 2,000 years. Their gait is distinctive and is high stepping and free, like that of a horse. They are able to run at top speed with a double suspension gallop, which is outstanding and beautiful to watch. They can achieve a top speed of up to 25 miles per hour. Although, this is slow compared to that of other greyhound racing dogs, which can reach up to 45 miles per hour. Their color coat is a blue grey, black, red and fawn. Chance was a blue grey color. The Italian Greyhound makes an exceptional companion dog and loves the company of people. However, their slim build does make them somewhat fragile, and injury can result from rough or careless play with children. They are best with the elderly or a couple without any children for it prefers a quiet household. They love to run, obviously, therefore it is best to have them out of the city, but the older retired greyhound does well in the city. As for being a watchdog, they are great, as they bark at any unfamiliar sounds, however, they should not be considered a "true" guard dog as they are often aloof with strangers and easily spooked to run!

Spirit took to Chance immediately, as Spirit was a runner, from four previous generations of race dogs, she was born to run! And meeting Chance would give her the opportunity of a life time.

The poodle is the national dog of France, and the French sure do love their poodles, especially the large flamboyant "Standard", known as the

"French Poodle". However, in France, poodles are known as the Caniche, or "duck dog." The breed originated as a duck hunter in Germany, they called the poodle, a "pudelin", meaning a dog which splashes in water (for ducks). The "Standard" Poodle began its development as a retrieving water dog more than 400 years ago. They have a superlative swimming ability, and off-the-chart intelligence, and learning ability. Ranked second most intelligent dog breed behind the "Border Collie", according to the American Kennel Club.

The perfect poodle will have more of a square appearance, with longer hind legs than front, great for speed! A miniature poodle is under 15 inches in height, Spirit was 10 inches tall and weighed 10 pounds, later in life 11 pounds.

Well to say the least, Spirit and Chance were fairly equal in size, Chance was older and retired, but he could still run fast! Those two loved to visit in Bill's office, then he would take then out to the feed lot area, where he had a long strip parallel to the thousands of cattle. Guess the cattle were used to Chance chasing the cats and running the strip, as they stopped watching the dogs so much, once they started to run. I noticed Chance and Spirit would get to a certain end point, after running about 150 feet, appearing to turn around at the same time and run back. If Chance only ran 100 feet, Spirit would copy him.

They seemed to run at the exact same speed, so couldn't tell who was faster. It was more like they ran together at the same speed, as friends, not competitively.

On a later trip, Spirit and I showed up at the feed lot, and Bill had put a marker up for Chance, to turn around at the piece of wooden board, which he had nailed to the feed lot fence post. Which Bill said was about 150 feet, as he had previously figured. Bill had a pocket timer, like they used at the Greyhound Speed Way where Chance retired from. Both Chance and Spirit were well trained to sit and stay, until we said "GO", or return at the whistle. We used the whistle for them to return on a shorter run, than the fence post. Bill explained that 300 feet round trip for Chance, was equivalent to less than 200 yards, or about one-half a furlong, or one fourth of a mile round trip. I said, not bad for an old hound dog retired. Bill said let's get them to the start line and run them together, they both love to race, let's see which one is faster. Sounded like a plan to me and fun for Spirit for sure.

We lined Spirit and Chance together at the start line. Chance seemed to know this was different, Spirit just followed instructions to stay when told to stay at the start line. Spirit knew she was going to get to run, but did not seem to know this was a race of competition, as she was never trained to actually race to win the race! She just loved to run! When Bill yelled "GO", they both took off seeming at the same time, running side by side to the fence post, never looking any direction only forward, both running full speed together, arriving at the finish line together! I asked Bill who won? He said Spirit! I replied, it looked like they both finished at the same time to me. He said they did! But only because Spirit slowed down on the turn for my old greyhound! I asked what was their time? Bill said, 21 miles per hour, a bit fast for just a companion pet!

Well, needless to say, Chance was retired and would never actually race in competition again, and as for Spirit, I would only let her run for fun, never competition. She never stopped running, the house and yard were her sphere of eminent domain, I learned to stand very still for the 60 seconds, when she ran! Bought a bike and ran her, rather than walk her around the neighborhood.

CHAPTER III

Compassionate Services of Love

I did not buy Spirit to show or race, I had a perfect show dog with racing ability. I never considered breeding her either, even with her 5 generations of being a unique "Phantom Poodle Pedigree", as she was for me a companion and best friend.

Before mom passed away, she had issues with a bad knee and fell in the kitchen. She broke her hip, which caused her to need more help than I could provide at home any longer. This is when Spirit and I began our visits to see the elderly and sick in rest homes as a team together. A Hospice area was also in this rest home, in North Scottsdale, Arizona.

Spirit was allowed to visit with me, as well join us in the dining room every day for lunch. She was trained not to take treats or food, so she was no problem in the dining room. She was so well behaved that the facility allowed her to visit everyone that wanted to be visited. Spirit was never a trained "therapy" pet, she did not wear a therapy type leash. But pets are welcome in most rest homes if you are invited to visit with certain residents. We were invited so often our visits became routine. Spirit loved waving to individuals for a petting session, she could do this for hours. She also loved anything with wheels, so she took to the baby grand piano in the lobby as soon as she saw it moved across the room! Spirit took to all the folks sitting in wheel chairs as well, in the lobby, and dining room, in their rooms, wherever she saw wheels and people to pet her, which was 98% of the residents! Mom was a music teacher most of her life, taught piano as well as voice. To entertain the residents, I would remove the piano bench and place moms wheel chair in place of the piano bench, up to the baby grand piano. She played and I sang to the audience, while Spirit took turns letting everyone come to her chair to pet her, as she waved them hither. Sometimes she would sit in their laps, knowing she would get a ride back to their rooms with them, wheels, ride! She was soft, gentle and every so careful sitting with the residents. She never jumped from their laps, as she knew to wait and be removed by me.

Those were some of the happiest days of our lives, because to show compassion to the lonely, sick, old and dying, is a satisfaction within itself! A love you feel you shared with others, Spirit's love, was so special to them. The gratitude shown, and tears of joy those elderly souls had towards us, was our reward, their gratitude would have made angels cry!

My heart ached for so many of them because they never had anyone visit them, as I was there every single day and saw this. I had spent years doing compassionate services on my own without Spirit, but with her it was so much better. Spirit had a habit of waving to everyone who would look at her! This was her way of asking to be petted, but I believe she also felt somehow it was a duty of kindness she was born to deliver! Even the employees would smile and pet her, she never got tired of waving, and riding in wheel chairs! She seemed to know what everyone needed to make them happy, and happy they were, to pet such a special friend.

Spirit was amazing, how she would look directly into the aging eyes of each individual resident, then wave at them. They felt she was being very personal, and she was. Even saying goodbye, Spirit would look at the person, as I held her, wave three or four times, then look at another individual, repeating her waving in the same matter, until she was tired. I knew when she was tired because her waves became only, two and three waves, then one and two waves. But, she never gave up, until I took her out of the building. The residents would ask, when will you come see me again, so often with tears in their tired old eyes. It was always difficult to leave some of the residents without Spirit personally having greeted them, but she always waved goodbye to the entire group as we departed out of the lobby door, as this is where they often met with us, to hear mom play the piano, or just visit, before they would all be wheeled back to their rooms. Of which would be the same routine day after day after day, hoping for a visit from a friend or family, which rarely appeared!

It seemed this was Spirits destiny or karma in life, to be of service, this was Spirits virtual world! She served a needed service to these souls in need, something we both could feel with all our senses! The eyes saw the needs, the ears heard the pleads, Spirits soft touch with her paws, often brought shameless tears to their aged eyes. The shame I thought to myself, was the neglect and failure of the children to visit their elderly, as some of these individuals never saw anyone, until their funerals!

I wondered why our creator allowed so much wrongfulness, pain and suffering, in this world! Then I answered myself, I figured it is all about being tested! Some creatures and humans have to suffer, that others might be tested. I think when any animal is treated cruel, it knew before it was born, it's destiny was to be used to test a human, it came her to earth for a purpose, for our needs. When this animal's soul (yes they have souls), goes over Rainbow Bridge, it will be one of the strongest and most valiant spirits on the other side of the veil. Same with humans, our tests depend on our valence in our previous existence of eternal rounds.

I believe we grow eternally, as who or what we are, as ourselves, an animal, plant or tree. Not as a different reincarnated individual, animal or plant, not as someone else, but eternally in existence, as an intelligence, with physical bodies for the purpose of being in the world. Our refined spiritual bodies I believe, will be visible when the time comes, like the stars seen at night, disappear when the sun shines.

This is reason to believe we will be re-united with our animals when we cross over. This gives us faith and hope, something to believe in, otherwise for what reason would we bother to even exist at all! Maybe the vast universes have or had life on many other planets such as ours, stands to reason, after all, just looking at the birth of a pet, a baby, a tree, a flower proves within itself, to be a miracle of a higher power, that has no beginning or end, rather an eternal round, like the circle! Cut the ring and break this circle, you will still have no beginning or end! We now watch the stars, billions and trillions of them, someday we will soar the heavens among those stars, what an exalted majestic thought! And, we will be re-united with our beloved pets, friends and families, if so desired. I believe our creator gives each of us our hearts desires, and by our lives, actions and works we create a place for ourselves in the eternal round. We make choices while in this world, which will cause for ourselves, our destiny, in the endless, eternal, immeasurable time!

Animals are here for our benefit, to serve our needs. We are to take care of them, it is our duty to be kind, not cruel, cruelty is inhuman, a sin, you set your destiny eternally!

CHAPTER IV

The Mystical Guest At Anne's House

Not only did Spirit have a full life visiting rest homes, and hospice centers, she befriended those who were sick, or dying in their homes. Such was the case with the neighbor across the street from our home, her name was Anne, she was in her 80's and dealing with health issues.

From the day Spirit came home with me, she was the "cats meow", a fluffy soft ball of fur, with a loving personality, to most the neighbors. Especially to Angie and Anne.

Angie Spirit adored, and loved visiting, as this was a close friend of mine. Angie lived a few blocks from us, so we would take the "wheels" to visit her, a ride, a ride, take me on a ride, she expressed, waving at me repeatedly. I knew where she wanted to go, down to the lake, less

than a mile from the house, to feed "Rocky"!
Rocky was an old white duck Spirit had
befriended, next to the Chart House Restaurant.
Rocky was amazing! He couldn't fly with his
friends, so he floated alone, when they flew away.
When Spirit would show up to visit Rocky, the
duck, we would sometimes fed him, Rocky would
actually run to us when we called him, literally
running on top of the water. Quack, quack,
quacking, as he approached us with his whacky,
waddling, waggling, cute little self! Across the
grass, into the parking lot, which overlooked
the lake, on McCormick Ranch, in Scottsdale,
Arizona.

Of course on the way home Spirit would
always look towards Angie's house, as if to say,
hey mom, look, Angie lives right there, let's go to
her house! Spirit loved her visits to see Angie, as
Angie always let her have run of the house, her
favorite haunt was Angie's closet! I don't think
either of us ever figured that one out! When
Angie was sick we enjoyed cooking up a get well
soup to deliver to her front door. Seems Spirit
learned and understood the difference between
door delivery of food, from friendly visits. She
knew, when mom leaves food at any front door,
someone is sick! She knew the difference and
patiently waited in the car on these type rides,
called meals on wheels.

Annie, was really close, across the street, but Spirit was trained never to cross any street alone, so she was never a problem running over to Anne's without me. But, I knew when she wanted to visit Anne, as she would sit under the big pine tree in front and just stare at Anne's house. Anne was very busy for an 80ish old lady, and lady she was. She had traveled the world many times with her late husband who had been a doctor until he retired. She often told me about her wonderful home on top of a mountain, how happy she was in that home. I asked her why she moved to this humble small home in our HOA! She said 7,000 sq. ft. was too large, as they were older and figured 2,000 sq. ft. was big enough. So she and her husband, Ed, moved together into the home across the street. Ed was still working, as he had not yet retired, he had a beautiful office in his home, which had beautiful wood cabinets for his medical library, with a large desk of mahogany wood, his chair was brown leather with a high back and leather arms.

Annie had moved into her home before I lived in mine, so I never met her husband, as he had passed away before I moved to the neighborhood. In fact, we never really talked about his passing until the day Spirit and I went to visit Anne.

Anne had a "yellow" chair made of satin, which she placed in her den to watch TV. The den was on the front of her home, next to the kitchen, so we seldom used the living room, unless she was having a big dinner party, which she often had since she was well know in her own circle, as a design artist for flowers, winning International awards. I felt lucky, to be sometimes invited to her functions. We moved in different circles, but one thing we shared in common was Spirit! She took to her like a duck to water.

When Spirit and I would visit with Anne, Anne always sat in her yellow chair, which was big enough for her and Spirit to share. Spirit would sit for a half hour or so, then act like she wanted to get down and look around. Anne allowed her the run of the house, like Angie did. Anne and I would visit and talk, as Spirit snooped around. We knew Spirit would not make a mess, as she was trained well, to ask to go bye bye. As for chewing or breaking things, it never happened anywhere. She liked to smell and look at everything, but her intellect told her what was the wrong things to do! Anne suggested Spirit was so smart, that I have her IQ tested, she said her friend at the Arizona University does this testing of animals. I never did that since it didn't really matter anyway, she was my pet, served my purpose without being tested for her IQ.

Being at Anne's tonight would prove to be different! Anne and I decided to sit in the living room by the fire place and chat. Here we could get a better view of what and where Spirit was snooping around. Anne had to go to the bath room and decided to use the one in her late husband's office, which was actually built to be the master bed room, so it had a bath room area, with a closet, still with some of her late husbands clothing. His desk still had his personal items where he left them before he died.

Anne returned to the living room with a shocked look on her face. I wondered if Spirit did something wrong. I asked, where is Spirit? Anne said, you have to come with me, you have to see this! I got up and followed Anne to her late husband's office! My mouth fell to the floor, I said, I wonder how long she has been sitting there! Anne said, I don't know, but it is strange, as the last person to sit in that chair was Ed! Anne said, I have goose bumps, I feel my husband's presence, I believe Spirit is mystically connected somehow, to departed spirits! My mouth still wide open, I called Spirit to follow us and sit by the fire place, spending the rest of the evening thinking about what had happened.

As time passed and more visits were made, Anne and I noticed Spirit often took leave and walked to the office to sit in Ed's chair. We both at times would join her, standing in that room, never sitting, just standing and waiting for Spirit to jump down and join us, which was generally fifteen minute visits! Anne insisted

we never disturb Spirit by asking her to move
from the chair. Anne always whispered with me
when we joined Spirit, asking me to whisper
as well, most of the time I just looked at Ed's
enormous collection of books, from all over the
world, on his library shelves. Often reading the
notes he had made in many of those books. Anne
enjoyed my interest in her late husband's life and
adventures, explaining the medical speaking
engagements he had, while visiting various
countries. I felt more and more connected to
Ed and his life, reading his notes, feeling "his"
virtual world! Ed was still sharing his world
with us! Spirit had actually brought Ed back
to life for Anne, she was so happy, at peace,
she often declared! Ed was watching over her,
now as a guardian angel, even I was plausibly
convinced of this. To see an elderly old woman,
with pains from age, just smile, was a gift to
me, I was happy, to see Anne happy, always so
excited about Ed's visits!

When Spirit walked to Ed's office, Anne would
smile and say, how nice, Ed is here tonight, look
"Spirit knows", Ed is with us tonight, I wonder if
Spirit can see him! Somehow I felt this was ok,
as Anne seemed happy to feel Ed's spirit was
still with her, as her guardian angel. Sometimes
Anne would walk over to Ed's desk, where Spirit
sat, in Ed's chair, and pick up an object which
she and Ed had purchased in a far away country

together. Anne would hold the miniature statute, paper weight or other such objects from his large desk, touching them ever so affectionately, at times talking to Ed, with such fond memories, she would exclaim, we had a wonderful life, didn't we Ed?! I often wondered if he answered her, I think she could hear him say, yes we did, and one day we will be together again.

Funny thing, but I often felt those strange cold chills, or electricity going through my body as well! Maybe it was true, Spirit had a special connection. After all she did the same thing at our house, after mom passed away! She would now and then go into the back bed room, where my mom spent most of her last years, bed bound. After mom passed away, I turned out the lights, shut the drapes, and put a long life light bulb into mom's night light candle, which was on her dresser. Moms light still burns even to this day, in memory! Love is Eternal you know! So this keeps me going, to believe in things yet unseen! It is liken to, when you open a window at the break of dawn, the sunlight beams in, you can then see tiny particles, or minute subdivisions of matter, flickering like glow bugs, twinkling. Then as the ray of sun shine disappears, so does our ability to see the minute particles of matter, as our vision is not able to see this matter, minute particles, without the brightness of the suns rays. Just as the stars are in the sky, both in the day and at night, but our vision can only see these stars glowing at night. As during the day our earth's star, the Sun, makes our sky so bright that we cannot see the much dimmer stars, but they are still out there, throughout our universe, and beyond! I call this our second vision, as we can see at night, what we can't see during the day! It is a lot easier to see the glow of a candle in the dark than in the light. Maybe Spirit had her third vision, the ability to see what is unseen, like refined matter of souls departed! I believe she did, Anne believed she did!

As time passed, Anne was diagnosed with cancer, she suffered a lot, so our visits became more frequent. As fate takes its turn with all of God's creation, life as we know it in this world ends. Anne knew her time was near its end, she was very wealthy and could afford lots of home care, she wanted to die at home she told me and arranged to do just that! She had a hospital bed moved into her den, where her dinette set once was. Her TV and yellow chair remained in the same place, within her site. Her green couch was on the right wall. Anne wanted to die like she lived, near things and memories she loved, she had previously told me she did not want to die in a rest home, if at all possible. She had everything arranged with her attorney(s) to make sure her wishes would be carried out accordingly.

Anna had arranged for hospice care in her home a few months prior to her falling into a coma. I wanted to take Spirit for a final visit before she passed away, even though Anne was in a comma. I asked the two caretakers if we could see Anne. It was already dark, but Spirit hadn't seen Anne in a few days, and seemed to want to go over to Anne's house that evening! I wanted Spirit to understand why she wouldn't be going back again, and this trip would explain it to Spirit. I do believe Spirit had already figured out that Anne would not be with us much longer, this was why Spirit seemed persistent for me to open the front door! When I opened the door, she ran directly towards Anne's house, stopping at the street, looking back, waiting for me, panting anxiously, appearing distressed, and rather in a hurry to get to Anne.

Spirit had worked with a lot of terminally ill patients, as I had, this would be no different, we would say our goodbyes, holding tender memories of friends we had made in Spirit's, as well as my, world. A world which kept getting smaller and smaller, with so many passing away.

The two young hospice girls were sitting with Anne since noon. Their shift would end as soon as the new staff showed up. One of the young ladies, which answered the door, spoke broken English, as she spoke Spanish. Spirit became totally calm once the door opened! The young lady said, I am the new girl, my name is "Juanita". I told Juanita it was alright to speak Spanish, as Spirit and I both understood her language. The other young lady with Juanita, was named Collette. The girls knew me as, Peg, the friend across the street, and Spirit, as a friend of Anne's also. They knew Anne was close to Spirit, because Anne always wanted to see Spirit when ever possible and had expressed this to all the hospice teams, before she fell into the coma. Thus, they allowed visits to see Anne, until the last moment of Anne's life in this physical world!

On this last visit, after having entering Anne's home, I picked Spirit up and held her in my arms this time. Spirit understood this was different, she no longer had the free run of Anne's home, she became calm and quiet, she knew this was the "special" visit! Anne was in a hospital bed, high off the floor, with arms on each side. She was still in a coma, as we approached her bed side, and just stood for several minutes next to her, I whispered to Anne several times, "Anne, Spirit is here to see you". The girls said there had been no change, Anne had been this way for days. I continued to stand next to the bed, holding Spirit in my arms. Anne's head was turned away from us, she appeared asleep. Spirit remained quiet and still in my arms. All of a sudden, Anne turned her head towards us, to her right side, looking directly at Spirit! Anne smiled at Spirit, she said, "Spirit", nothing more, just "Spirit"! Anne then lifted her right arm up to try to touch Spirit! Anne did not seem to see me, she never looked at me or anywhere else, only focused on Spirit! Juanita and Collette were observing all that transpired between Anne and Spirit. Spirit quickly sat up in my arms, giving Anne four animated waves with her tiny front paws, then stopped, as Anne gently touched Spirit's left paw. Anne lowered her left arm, shutting her eyes, with a beautiful peaceful smile on her face. Spirit's little paws went limp onto my arms. I knew Spirit knew! We were both very sad!

Juanita and Collette were in shock, they started to cry, as they walked us to the front door, saying, Spirit waved goodbye to Anne! Anne woke up just to say goodbye to Spirit, didn't she, the girls asked!

I thanked these young ladies for the wonderful services they did for our friend and neighbor, Anne. Spirit knew also, it was the end of seeing our dear friend, Anne, ever again, not in this physical world anyway! The next day the girls called me and said Anne had passed away.

Spirit, nor I, ever went back into Anne's home again, as it stayed vacant for years. I knew she missed seeing Anne, and Ed, so did I, very much!

As time passed, Anne's home was sold, but we realized the new neighbor did not welcome pets, so we stayed away, from what would always remain to us, "Anne's" house!

Now, Spirit and I had bigger fish to fry! Off to a new world of adventure!

Chaz & Spirit
"Daddy's Little Girl"

CHAPTER V

Daddy's Little Girl

After years of working with so many needy individuals, I figured it was time for Spirit and I to just enjoy life, traveling and being with friends who could do things together with us, as well as find a husband!

I gave up on married friendships. I was never single minded, but had a few single girl friends, as they are hard to find, they get married, name changes, then, they are gone like the wind, unlike male friends, they keep their names, so you can find them. One of these girl friends, which was a great animal lover, was Faith. Faith had moved to Arizona to take care of her dear uncle, who had a home on the lake near my home, he was ill, she was doing what I had done for years. Faith and I met at a pet store checking out our many doggie goodies. We shared petting one another's pets, talked and exchanged phone numbers. Faith was such fun, she had a beautiful dog named Bella, which had puppies. She was living 5 minutes from me, so I decided Spirit had so many toys, we would give Faith some for her new family. Bella had four new babies. Faith named one "King Mack", named after a road, in Detroit, Michigan. The man who she gifted King Mack to was Jewish, so he changed the dogs name to Isaac! Faith, with a giggle, exclaims, he made the puppy Jewish! The second puppy was named "Queen Charlotte", she was gifted to a couple from Poland, they taught their puppy Polish! Then there was, "Soldier", Faith named him after after one of her uncles, who was a soldier. Soldier was gifted to a famous author in New York, who passed away! Then of course, the fourth puppy was "Bibi", which Faith kept for herself. Bibi is alive and well with Bella and Faith, living in California, enjoying life, as Faith and the babies moved back to California, after her beloved uncle had passed away. Faith and I spent many holidays together, for several years, being single, not fitting in at married couples homes is never easy, especially when you have no children, grandchildren! I was an only child, so I didn't even have a sister or brother to join on holidays. Most of my aunts, uncles, cousins, family, had passed away, or lived across the country, which I hadn't seen some in 30 plus years! Faith and

I enjoyed sharing our lives, holidays and our babies together, filling in a few of our years, living the single life. This would prove to be the beginning of a long friendship which continues to this day.

Faith never decided to marry, but I did remarry. After Faith moved back to California, I met my future husband, Chaz! We dated for a year before I asked him to marry me! We laugh to this day about that! Chaz knew I never liked being single, hated it! He also knew from the first date that I was literally looking (and interviewing) for a husband! One that my dog could also learn to love! I had dated a number of gentlemen, but none seemed to be equally yoked. After years of being alone, I figured it was time to make a few concessions regarding my, "over the wall expectations in a man"!

A few concessions, yes, but I had a few requirements as well, that had to be equally yoked. One was Spirit! I never told Chaz, just watched him with her, how he treated her, how she reacted to him, watching him each visit, to see if he was really sincere about his love for dogs, which was part of his own life. Another requirement was a must, no criminal background! Another was trust and loyalty, which, now after nine years of marriage, I have to say, I trust that he would take a bullet for me, loyal for sure! Now the criminal background of any man was a serious concern I had about dating any new person.

Chaz had lots of proof that he had worked as a sales representative most of his life, was successful enough. Although I could care less about his financial worth, I required he could cover his financial needs to survive in the world, which he could do.

He had served two years in the U.S. Army, during the Vietnam War. (A little history here on Vietnam – it is note worthy to know that Vietnam's recorded history stretches back to the mid-to-late 3rd century BC. Pre-historic Vietnam was home to some of the world's earliest civilizations and societies, making them one of the world's first people who practiced agriculture and rice cultivation. The Red River valley formed a natural geographic and economic unit, bounded to the north and west by mountains and jungles, to the east by the sea and to the south by the Red River Delta.

Chaz was a Veteran of the "Nan" era. I liked the fact he had served our nation, as most my family had also. He told me he was an expert shot as well. I liked this, since I was as well! This would be the final test! At the gun club! Before we married, I enrolled us in a class together to get certified to carry weapons, yep, to cause him to be fingerprinted! But Chaz didn't know that was why! I knew if he was clean, he could get his CCW permit.

I was cleared within a week, but I had an FBI clearance years ago, because I had worked for the criminal intelligence, CIS, for the State Police. My fingerprints were on file. Chaz's prints did not receive a clearance! He received a letter, stating to go to the police department and be re-printed! Oh no, I thought, this is going down badly!

Then I remember watching Chaz get printed, I remembered they did not print him well, as I was an expert at finger printing, I saw his prints were blurred. The gun club had arranged for someone to print all of us at the club, they had send the prints to the FBI for us. I knew my prints were ok, because I relaxed and help the gal to roll my fingers properly, viewing them they looked perfect! I noticed, Chaz did not do this, as I had watched him get printed! I viewed his prints as well, I noticed they were not clear enough to read properly. I told Chaz this had to be the issue! I hoped this was the issue! I wanted a "daddy" for Spirit, and a hubby, was tired of dating!

Chaz was re-printed and cleared for take-off, or I should say cleared for his CCW permit! Bingo! I believed, I had finally found myself a husband! Now, I hoped we could agree to fly together! Really fly, a plane that is! Well, that wasn't so successful! Chaz refused to fly together with me, as I was the pilot! So he sat with Spirit, at the Scottsdale Air Park and waited for me to return! Once, he waited for me to fly to Sedona, Arizona and return, he said the ballgame was on at the Air Park, so not a problem. Small negative, as I made my approach on landing the runway, I waved my wings to him, like hello, I'm back, but he never even watched for my superwoman landing! Well, he isn't impressed easily, that's alright, neither am I, so we're equally yoked on that one! Bingo! He is patient, he would need that with my personality, and our high spirited "Spirit"! Big plus!

After a year of dating, Chaz and I married, having a nice cake, and a big fat church wedding, with all those married couples that rejected me while single! Chaz was not of my faith, he was a Roman Catholic, as my parents were also, I was fine with this. He knew his religion well, as well as scriptures, put me to shame! In the following nine years of marriage I would discover that I had married a genius! His IQ was off the wall, his ability to remember dates of events in history, world wide events, from four corners of the world, was shocking to me. He had a memory unsurpassed, of religion and history. I could ask him dates, names, events around the world, he knew! Chaz was faster than asking "Siri", I loved a challenge, he would prove to be just that.

Now I had found my match, a smart husband and a smart dog, both seemed to outsmart me most of the time! This would be another new adventure, the three of us, in our very own world, growing, learning, traveling this journey together.

Chaz literally fell in love with his, as he came to call her, "Little Girl", sometimes he called her, "Baby Girl". I called her Spirit mostly, but at times I also called her "Baby Girl", was after all, my little boy's name that had passed away, Baby, who Spirit adored. Spirit related to all three names, so this worked out well.

Spirit loved to learn and Chaz loved to teach. She learned to count, add, subtract. This was done with training, with treats. As were her obedience and behavior modification classes. In those classes I used treats, as well as a spray bottle with water, using a light mist, sprayed into her face when she moved from her square. We rarely used the water bottle at home, as she was very hurt emotionally if sprayed. She would go to her bedroom, in the closet. This is where she would go when she didn't feel well, as it was dark and quiet, and large, a walk-in closet. We never shut the door, or ever needed to shut her in. Spirit was always free to leave the closet when she desired, she would wait until called, if punished, which was extremely rare. Running out the front door was a closet punishment, she did that once, after Anne died, she ran out the door, crossed the street to go see Anne, but remained at her walk-way until I picked her up and brought her home. That was so sad, because I punished her for that, for her wanting to see her friend so bad that she broke all the rules, which she never did again!

Counting was interesting, it would come it handy in the years to come!

Counting was usually done in the kitchen area, as her treats were on a tray with "wheels", she loved that treat tray and could pull it out herself when she wanted a treat. We allowed her to do that, but she was not allowed to take anything from the tray, she had to ask. She taught us that one bark meant follow me, two barks meant, let me out the back door. Then she had tones and pitch for one bark and two barks. Daddy would reach for a bag of treats and say, as he held it up, this one Little Girl, if that was the wrong choice, he would try another bag, until she barked once with a certain tone and pitch, as to say yes. Sometimes she would walk over to the tray and pick her bag with her nose. For new treats she was not familiar with, we would put two bags opened on the floor, she would then sniff them both and pick with her paw the one she wanted that day.

Chaz started telling Spirit to go sit on the carpet in the dining room, off the kitchen area, where her square dinner napkin was for her dinner bowl. She had learned about the square, this was a square to work from. She sat next the the square dinner napkin until Chaz would say, "come to daddy". Spirit would take off at high speed, sit and wait for daddy to say, "is this what you want", waiting for her answer. Yes, was a loud single bark. Finally, he had her sitting at by her square counting! He would tell her to stay, as he counted from one to three, then tell her "OK". He repeated this procedure until she had learned to wait until the count of 8. She knew not to move at 6 or 7, or daddy would say no, hold his hand out, telling her to go back to her square and start over. We never pushed her pasted 8 because it became work, not fun and this was a pet not a work dog!

She enjoyed learning and I am sure she could have gone to fifty, because she was trained to jump 50 times each day to the sink level. This was accomplished by giving her squeaky toy a bath, she had to do her 50 jumps to get the toy. As she grew older we had to reduce the jumping, as we noticed her running less. Poodles are known to have issues with their hips, but we hoped the exercises would prolong her bone issues. I believe it did, as she still ran the house until she was 14 years old, which was in February 2nd, 2018.

Spirit was so smart that she never stopped surprising us! We had to think up new games all the time to keep up with her brilliant, curious mind. One advanced game she like was using her intelligent mind to figure out how to untie a square blanket, which had first been rolled, with her squeaky toy in the center. We did a few video of the amazing way she did this. Since the toy was rolled into the blanket first, then tied into a knot, she had to first untie the knot. Spirit would place her nose into the center of the knot, use her paws to pull as she used her nose to push the knot open. She had to work at this for a few minutes, as we did not make this easy, the knot was fairly tight. She then lay the rolled blanket out and with her nose unrolled the blanket for the toy.

Another fun game to watch her play, was Beep Beep. Chaz named the game, because he taught her how to play. It was hide and seek. She would bring him a squeaky toy, he would toss it, she would retrieve, but he added a trick. He would play like he tossed it, tell her to retrieve it, but she had to find it, as she didn't see him toss it. She would look under the chair for example, he would say beep beep, to Spirit that was a no. At the sound of beep beep she looked like a prairie dog with those stops and head turns, each time he would say beep beep. With each beep beep she make sharp turns to go to the next hiding place, until she found the squeaky toy, which daddy had tossed in the other direction when he had her looking in another direction. It was a game that went on night after night for years. We always enjoyed it together, as she was so pretty to watch.

Spirit had one game she played alone when we didn't want to play. She would put her squeaky on one side of bedroom door, slam the door shut, then put her paws, like a cat, under the door and pull the toy under the door until she got it on the other side! This was really amazing, since she had to figure out the distance she would have to pull the toy under the door, her paws had to be able to reach that distance. If that weren't enough, she picked sizes of toys that she could pull easily, even learning the texture of each toy. She knew if they were too thick they would not work, if too big, they would not work. It was obvious she had a mathematical mind more than all my previous dogs, Chaz agreed, she was the smartest dog he ever knew. This was hard to capture on a video since she would shut the door! Shutting doors became her way of getting our attention as well. She would lock herself into the bedroom and we had to get up from a nice movie to open the door, this worked well for her, attention or I'll do it over and over until you see me! We knew she would give up after an hour or so, it was good exercise anyway, so we continued to get up and open the door for as long as it took.

The other thing Spirit liked to do at home, was dance. To her dancing was me holding her upside down like a rag doll and dancing to slow music. She only danced with me, as she knew I knew just how to hold her upside down, with her head hanging down as she lay limp in my arms. What a love bunny!

We did a lot of traveling for years, but became more and more content being home. Being home was actually wonderful! We both loved to cook, and Chaz was a great cook. He was Italian, so pasta and sauce were his middle name! As he cooked he spoke Italian to Spirit, she became Italian and understood his commands in Italian! Spirit also loved to travel, so I would go to the market and take her with me, she would take a nap while waiting in the car. If we were at a pet store, she would bark a block away, knowing we are going for a ride in a shopping cart. If I turned the other direction, she cried to tell me to turn around. The memory she had amazed us all the time.

Being married had its bad days and good days, as all marriages, but as Chaz said, marriage is a matter of "compromise, arbitration, concessions," and a firm committal to endure to the end, in good times and in bad times!

I "Do", is the most important word you will ever say in your life. After all, I do, means, you will! I have few regrets in life, but Chaz is not one of them! I am grateful he became the best "daddy" in the world to Spirit, "Daddy's Little Girl"!

TO EVERY THING THERE IS A SEASON,

And a time to every purpose and
matter under the heaven:

A time to be Born

A time to Die

A time to weep, and a time to laugh,

A time to mourn, and a time to dance

Heavens Portal

CHAPTER VI

Spirit's Rainbow Bridge to Heaven's Portal

Born
February 2, 2004
Died
July 26, 2018

Spirit taught me that animals deserve respect and care. She helped me understand that animals are a unique creation, which live by instinct, but in my opinion, Spirit also had reasoning, many animals show reasoning abilities. I believe she also had a more acute awareness of spiritual reality than we realized, but no ability to tell us by God's design. But observation, told Anne, and myself as well, she could see things unseen! For what reason, it does not matter!

Most people in the world believe in a "Supreme Being", most believe in the the story of Noah and the ark, in Genesis (which means origin or source), is the first book in the Bible. Which talks about the creation of the world and all in it. The story of Noah explained how the animals were called into the ark by God. When the flood began, the animals "went into the ark to Noah", as God drew them to the ark, God communicated with them directly. It is therefore certainly "plausible" that God interacts with animals more than we realize, not that He is communicating with animals all the time, no more than with humans, with a free agency to choose.

By their very existence animals are as much the product of God's creative energy as any other part of creation. We should respect animals and all God's creation, having a love for them, caring for them. They have the capacity to enjoy life, as mentioned in (Job 39:13), the ostrich flapping its wings "joyously", and the beasts of the field "playing" in their surroundings (Job 40:20). We should not take away the joy of animals, for there is an eternal price tag for being cruel to them, as they are beings with a soul, with the capacity for joy. Animals will be the co-inheritors with us of the new creation, in heaven. In Isaiah 11:6-9, the prophet Isaiah saw a day when humans and animals would live once again in perfect harmony, this is a vision of the eternity. We will see our beloved animals again where the rose continues to grow and spread its scent so sweet. Why not? It is a moot question!

Rainbow Bridge For Our "Little Girl"

Spirit had to leave us very recently. Chaz and I had to make a hard decision, a decision many of you may have to make someday, when your beloved pet grows old, sick and terminally ill.

You will have to figure out what to do. I don't like to remember those weeks of having to make that decision, as it pierces and wounds my heart to recall. The pain, is like a dart into my heart, to see her and then, no-more, she's gone in a heart beat, less than a second.

But for the sake of allowing any animal a peaceful departure from this physical world, I would like to take this opportunity to share with you Spirits last weeks of life here.

Spirit had a wonderful 14th, birthday, February 2, 2018, she was even running fast like a young puppy, but not as long as the years before, what she did for 10 minutes was now a run for only 30 seconds. She had lost 90% of her vision within the last few years and 98% of her hearing in the past year. But she had learned the home well, still ran deaf and 90% blind, but could see shadows. Her own shadow on the wall would appear as she walked to her bathroom in the evenings. We had placed motion detectors with lights to help her to jump up and down from her bed, and follow the lights as they would detect her motion. She did well. Even as sick as she had become, she loved to hang her head out the window to go for a ride.

Her last ride was to see her Veterinarian, who loves to help out with the zoo animals that become ill. I gave her medications for lots of medical issues. He could see she was not herself. For several weeks she tried to eat and walk, but her walking became painful, as she cried at times. We knew the life expectancy of her breed and size was 12 to 15 years. She was now 14 and ½ years old, this would leave only 6 more months, unless she were extraordinary!

Chaz could not even talk about the possibilities before us. I knew I would have to make this decision, one I had made 6 times in the past with my previous dogs. Therefore, I knew what was before me!

In the past I never used a doctor to help, by coming to the home, for hospice care or euthanasia. It was 5 times an emergency room situation, always after midnight, then the drive home alone without my pet, the tears trying to drive home. The last time was for Baby, he was having a heart attack at 2:00 AM, I was a widow then and mom was bed ridden, she waited up for me to return home at 4:00 AM. The task was traumatic! But I had a new puppy, Spirit, this made it easier to deal with, but the loss of a pet of 15 years is never easy, no matter how they leave you.

Spirit became strangely involved in returning to my mom's bedroom, where she slept when she was a little puppy. She would just go in there and sit, sometimes with her nose in the air, smelling, like she did at Anne's in Ed's office.

She showed all the signs of a dog who was in pain and discomfort, her breathing was obviously very hard. That is when I started to do research, which I did for almost two weeks before making any decisions. Hoping I could help her depart with uncompromising care and compassion. Her Veterinarian prescribed pain pills and sleeping medications, he knew what I was thinking, he knew where this was going, but allowed me to call the shots. I told his staff I would possible have Spirit's final moments be at home. This Veterinarian did not make house calls, so I called every one in town, checked them out with the State, to see if they were real Veterinarian's, without any complaint's filed against them.

I found a wonderful doctor, DVM, he was skilled in internal medicine, surgery, and emergency care, as well as hospice and home euthanasia. He had a staff of wonderful caring people who took lots of time on the phone to arrange a visit, to decide what to do, and for how long.

Hospice was already being done as far as I was concerned, Spirit was already on pain and sleeping medications. She had moved from her bed into the doorway of the "walk in" closet, which was a big signal to me! I could see her breathing was awful, appeared fluid was present, as her nose was dripping water. She wanted me to just hold her, looking into my eyes with her little blind eyes, not being able to see me, my heart was broken. She could still see shadows and feel my loving touch, as well as her "daddy's"!

Dr. Michael, arrived at 4:00pm with his assistant, a young lady with lots of compassion and understanding of what needed to be done. Dr. Michael explained his findings to me and my husband, it did not sound good, we could keep her alive maybe 2 or 3 more weeks. Chaz knew what I had decided, he had to leave the bedroom, as this is where we all were, on the floor with Spirit guiding her out of the closet door way. She followed me dragging her left leg, stopped at my foot stool, where she often was given a massage. She though she was going to get a massage, my heart was broken, I knew this would be the last place she would be in her final moments in our world. I felt so guilty, I tricked her, how cruel of me. But I knew she would not have the trauma of driving again to the Vet, or fearing what he would do. This helped me to do what I felt was the most humane thing I could do, eliminate the pain and suffering of my pet, waiting for the inevitable!

As Spirit sat on the foot stool, I pet her and kissed her, she was so tired looking, but still beautiful, I didn't want to let her go and no one pushed me to make this decision. The doctor said, I can return when "you" are ready. Me, I can't allow this to be about "me", I had to do this for her, I loved her! She was ready, I was not! I said it is time. His assistant gathered his bag and gloves for him. I gave Spirit her comfort by distracting her, as he injected a shot for only sleep, which would only be effective for a short time. So he had to have my cooperation to continue quickly. Spirit did cry a tiny bit from the injection in her hip, but she went to sleep immediately, he injected the final shot, she was asleep. My heart fell, as I knew there was no turning back, all I could do not was hope she could still hear me and know I loved her and hated doing this. She was gone! I asked Dr. Michael to allow me to hear her heart, as I wanted to make sure she was really gone, I had to know this to know that she would not suffer waking up. I wrapped her in her pink satin blanket and lay her on my bed. I called Chaz to come in to and verify no heart beat, I then picked her up and held her in the blanket, then Chaz held her. I gave her to Doc's assistant, as she carefully took her she said, I will take care of her tenderly.

Her ashes were returned to us within a week. We lit a candle which still burns in memory tonight.

I write this book in memory of a wonderful companion named Spirit, who gave her love to us unconditionally. And, also in hopes to help others find their way to help their beloved pets in their final moments, at home when possible.

Notes

Notes